SHIFTLESS

ESSENTIAL POETS SERIES 216

Canada Council
for the Arts

Conseil des Arts
du Canada

ONTARIO ARTS COUNCIL
CONSEIL DES ARTS DE L'ONTARIO

50 YEARS OF ONTARIO GOVERNMENT SUPPORT OF THE ARTS
50 ANS DE SOUTIEN DU GOUVERNEMENT DE L'ONTARIO AUX ARTS

Guernica Editions Inc. acknowledges the support of the Canada
Council for the Arts and the Ontario Arts Council. The Ontario Arts
Council is an agency of the Government of Ontario. We acknowl-
edge the financial support of the Government of Canada through
the Canada Book Fund (CBF) for our publishing activities.

SHIFTLESS

JANET FRASER

GUERNICA

TORONTO – BUFFALO – LANCASTER (U.K.)
2014

Michael Mirolla, editor
Guernica Editions Inc.
P.O. Box 76080, Abbey Market, Oakville, (ON), Canada L6M 3H5
2250 Military Road, Tonawanda, N.Y. 14150-6000 U.S.A.

Book design by Jamie Kerry of Belle Étoile Studios
www.belleetoilestudios.com

Distributors:
University of Toronto Press Distribution,
5201 Dufferin Street, Toronto (ON), Canada M3H 5T8
Gazelle Book Services, White Cross Mills,
High Town, Lancaster LA1 4XS U.K.

First edition.
Printed in Canada.

Legal Deposit – Third Quarter
Library of Congress Catalog Card Number: 2014934796

Library and Archives Canada Cataloguing in Publication
Fraser, Janet, 1954-, author
Shiftless / Janet Fraser. (Essential poets series ; 216) Poems.
Issued in print and electronic formats.
ISBN 978-1-55071-885-0 (pbk.).
--ISBN 978-1-55071-886-7 (epub).
--ISBN 978-1-55071-887-4 (mobi)
I. Title. II. Series: Essential poets series ; 216
PS8561.R2958S55 2014
C811'.6   C2014-900240-8   C2014-900241-6

CONTENTS

I. Conditions on the Avalon

Conditions on the Avalon	13
"A Refreshing Production Brought to You by Son-Rise"	16
Two Sisters	20
Grade Six Girls	22
Big-Headed	24
The Laws of Science	27
Highfield Road	29
Saint John	31
The River People	33
Wife: Glosa	35
Punished for Life	37
The Marriage Ghost	38
Her Daily Special	40
Dreams about Babies and Birds	41
The Heirs of Ethel Rosenberg	43
Tigers	45
The Distant Self	46
The Close Star	47

II. Some of the Women in my Tree: A Spoon Riverish Anthology

My Maternal Side	*51*
1. Mary Towne Easty (1634-1692)	51
2. Frances Everett Brown (1869-1952)	53

3. Marion Brown MacGowan (1901-1963)   54
4. Ruth MacGowan Fraser (1930-)   55
5. Patricia Fraser (1958-)   56

My Paternal Side   57
1. Georgina (Georgie) MacDonald Fraser (1862-1950) 57
2. Clarice Fraser (1905-1996)   58
3. Irenee Bedard Fraser Walker (1897-1992)   59
4. Irene Fraser Cunningham (1918-2005)   60

III. Boys and Men

The Golfers   63
Tall Tales   65
Two Triolets for Grandpa   67
Father and Son   68
How We All Start   69
Missing Boys   70
Fire   72
Lazy Days at the Psych Ward   73
Psychiatrist's Notes on Boy   74
The Game   75
Moose   76
Manning up to It   78
Trust/Tryst   79
Strap Across the Back   81
Hard of Hearing   83
The Missionary's Son   84
Bait and Tackle   86
Things I Loved   87
Occupations: A Picaresque   88
Windswept at Yonge and Bloor   90

IV. Self-Portrait

Self-Portrait	93
The One Who Stays	95
Child's Play	98
Best Friend	99
First Lover	101
Holiday	102
Our Reunion	104
Mother Love Poem	106
Don't Leave Me	107
Domestic Drama: Eight Prose Poems	108
Leaving Nova Scotia	112
ACKNOWLEDGEMENTS	115
ABOUT THE AUTHOR	116
PRAISE FOR THE AUTHOR'S *LONG GIRL LEANING INTO THE WIND*	117

To Christian and Alex

It was my goal always to be shiftless.
I saw the merit in that.

— Raymond Carver, "Shiftless"

I

CONDITIONS ON THE AVALON

Conditions on the Avalon

(Vignettes)

Tropical warning – high
windy gusts expected.
Isaac's eyewall will pass
eastern Newfoundland,
when warning
turns to watch.

*

Alma's late husband
came here from away
(late as ever).
Said this country
chilled his heart.
Left for Miquelon
with Black Horse
and Hard Tack.

*

Mary from Bay Bulls:
Mum took ill
when I were born.
Nerves rubbing
like sparks,
crucifix to her breast.
A life both fire and ashes.

*

The saltbox widow across
the lane turns 76, hosts her

17 children still living.
Fills jam jars with wild
white roses.
Picks her garden's
golden cloud berries.

＊

Yvonne leaves Town
for Northern Bay.
No one wants me
the whale of a woman
wails to her Nan. Last
seen on Shore Road,
headed for the landwash.

＊

Bride crooked from birth.
She's a quare hand
the lads say and throw her
off the wharf. Off to the
Waterford for the cure.
Most days she's down
to the docks
looking for the lads.

＊

Anna, rescued and raised
in Churchill Square.
Inuit girl rides her pony,
collects her ribbons.
At 16 a crackhead,
at 20 a cracked head.
Here lies Anna,
beloved daughter ...

*

Carmen dreams of pineapples,
fills herself with fire.
A dragon's flames on the sub-
Arctic acreage.
Covers carious rock
with red silk, lime chiffon.
Recalls
that first mustard crocus.

"A Refreshing Production Brought to You by Son-Rise"

I.

The first women Red Hatters
in veiled fedoras
full of bonhomie like
the welcome wagon women
who greeted my mother
at each new asylum
deep in suburbia.
Don't know Carroll's Mad
Hatter, but I recall
the Presbyterian hatmaker
in *Hatter's Castle*
who threw his pregnant
daughter out of the house
on Christmas Eve.
I read that book when 13
and an atheist, on my
best friend's mother's bed,
while her mom was out
partying with a married alderman.

2.

We follow the Hatters into
a Wesleyan slab,
rest on a plywood pew.
I wonder at the bold
ugliness of beige drywall
and carpet and strings
of red lights that remind

me of ambulances
when Miss Clavel
has a fright in the night.
Presumed rescued
like the rest
I'm mortified by my
strangeness (bashful spy
among the patriots,
no good at swaying and
lifting my eyes, can't sigh
and tear up when the
speakers hit their marks).
At Break a senior gives me
her business card
and invite to jewellery party.
She moves a limp wrist
away from me when I touch
her gold watch encrusted
with Swarovski crystals.

3.

I knew an evangelical lady
when I was a child.
God is Love and you were
Love, Mrs. Forest.
You were Love who loved
back an atheist
Presbyterian girl.
Love behind those swan-
necked glasses,
tied up with bobby pins,
in that slumped-down
Woolworth's dressed chest.
Love in the chattering of
the false teeth you took out

for me as a treat,
love when we warmed
ourselves over the floor vents.
You told me: "Don't say
good-bye dear. Say so long,
and then we'll meet again."
After you died I learned
your name was Flora. Flora,
my flowering forest friend,
I tried not to cry
that Christmas Eve Dad
and I visited you
in your dark freezing flat
on North Street, and gave
our good wishes to your
wino husband by the door.

4.

At Lunch a speaker sits at
our table. She was a gag
writer for Bob Hope and we
discuss the Hope-Woody
Allen connection.
At Music Hour I can't
bring myself to sing
the two-feet high words
on the movie screen
but take in *Evergreen*
and *I Will Always Love You*
as a guilty pleasure.
The production whimpers
when white-suited Gloria
reaches out to the broken-
hearted. For a bit of time
she makes me feel

Miss Clavel loves all
misbegotten Madelines.

5.

My evangelical friend
takes the wrong exit,
speeds past Spartan camps,
wide fields, ragged spruces.
We make the highway as
the red-rimmed sun gives
way, my friend humming
along with the hurtin'
parables on her CD player.
(Maybe she's thinking of
the husband who thumped
her out the door and how
she lost her boys that way.)

6.

Today I was a spy amidst
512 other women
in the House of Pentecost,
paying $123 for the visit
just as my parents paid
Flora Forest each year they
sojourned in New York.
So long, Mrs. F--, so long
even though you're not
looking down on me.
So long — Dear

Two Sisters

On the terrace
of the Restaurant Fournaise,
one hatted lady,
one flower-crowned girl.
Red and blue colour blocks
foreground green strokes.
Local models, not related,
for Renoir's *Two Sisters.*

She sent me that print
when we were freshly married.
I hung it by the picture window
of my garden room,
the one I retreated to nights
my husband stayed out.
(I didn't know her man
was a runabout too.)

As I grew up Renoir goddesses
fearlessly stared down at me.
Their rosy flesh, lustrous tresses,
corseted abundant dresses,
brightened the silent rooms
of three melancholy *femmes.*
(Two sisters and their mother
waiting for life to begin.)

Today my sister and I
don't speak of Art, or Mom,
a shy, gaunt artist who retired
after we were born, choosing
not to be a hobbyist,

settling for the Renoirs
that lived in our house —
the framed lush ladies.

Sis, good with her hands,
teaches school crafts
but is unwilling to take her
own oils into the light.
Her house is crammed with
Mom's discarded paintings,
all the tasteful fabrics
and porcelain she craves.

She lives with her daughter
in a mauve Victorian cottage.
Summers I visit her statuary
and formal gardens.
We sit on her polished verandah,
admire golden wire birdcages,
talk flatly for a bit
about our lives' surfaces.

Grade Six Girls

Now we're blonde, except
Linda who really was.
We look the same, we look
more ourselves, though
what we were then
is hard to understand.

✳

Laine, the one I admired,
whose admiring father waltzed
me round Lake Banook,
everyone watching.
Laine, who crumpled
my social standing to dust.

Faith taught me Go-Go,
banged on her Grand,
winced the times my mom
paid hers to watch me.
Forced good times and
rivalry wrenched us apart.

Sarcastic Sandra of the
sour looks, took me aside,
said it was wrong when
Mr. Lind smacked
Ann R. so hard she fell,
and what were we to do?

Marg, whose Scottish *mummy*
served tea and pie,
seemed not to know me

in junior high,
smoking in school corners
with new company.

Willow wisp Sal
of the deluxe split-level
invited me to parties
and desperate confidences,
tales of Mother's grace,
binge and purge.

Julie baked after school
at my house until
Mom kicked her out.
We didn't speak.
But I wanted to know
why I never saw *her* home?

Navy-brat Pat yawned
and got strapped by Mr. Lind.
Once she lent me all
her schoolgirl mysteries.
What went on in her red Colonial,
yard full of hounds?

❋

Grinning and slouching
we link arms for a reunion pic
that's as predictable as our
stiff, sad old class portrait.
Part of a time I'd long forgotten,
partially recall.

Big-Headed

(Photo, 1943)

My big-headed grandmother
stands feet apart
under an apple tree.
Broad shoulders straight,
hands held behind her back.
Her face looks down
at shady ground,
she does her best to smile.
Her wire-rimmed glasses
glint in the sun, magnify
her wide-set, long eyes.
Though her hair scraped
off a high forehead
is still brown,
and her belted dress
shows only a bit of a gut,
she's no longer the thin,
pretty young woman
who skated her way
into my grandfather's heart
and wed a widower,
an *unclean* man,
according to her parents

who wore black
to the ceremony.
It's war-time
and she's a widow
raising three children.
For the next 20 years
before she dies

she will not make love
to another man.
She will head
a construction crew
whose coarseness
depresses her.
She will tell my mother,
who slaps me
down for contrary opinions,
that it is good
I have a mind of my own,
unlike my cousin.
(Who still says and does
what her parents tell her
fifty years later.)

*

The last time I see her
it is Easter and she treats us
to a French restaurant!
I am seven,
dressed in the rainbow dress
she gave me,
trying to be good.
We eat her favourite, goose,
but she stutters, sighs,
angrily corrects.
I know that her big brain
that once translated Greek
is riddled by ratty moles,
yet she is trying to manage
my strange, raging mother
and my unreachable father
who's gone all white.
Big head, broad shoulders,
prettiness, my mother

and I inherited from her,
but not her steady modesty,
her wise efficiencies,
the bold, unflagging effort.

The Laws of Science

Memory wants rain.
  — Elisabeth Harvor

The trauma preacher
says fundamentally
hurt is one side
of a see-saw
we can pull down,
then push up the other side.
Thank our lucky stars
that can be seen
if we squint long
and hard enough.

Recall junior high
science and the physics
of bullying, our pull towards
boys and girls
who mock and curse us.
They create an opposite
and equal reaction
in the service
of a balanced operation.

With joy cost accounting
and sorrow gratitude,
because a girl learns
to love the dad who *incests*
her on her birthday
while the helium balloons
float graciously to the ceiling.

A teenage boy kills
himself, manifesting
a destiny determined
by age six.
Insults fuel us
like the fire
that dries up the rain,
floods the darkness.
Forget about death.
It's all good,
so get used to it.

Highfield Road

We're called Mommy
and Daddy when we arrive
with our two boys strapped
into the old Nova. We say:
"We're high on Highfield!"
Greet our new old house
at the top of the high field,
next to the little church
that praises Resurrection.

And next to the Ulster Arms
lot full of broken glass
and the KFC and Dairy Queen
and butcher shop alley where
a girl is raped and escapes
from a blond barbarian
called Paul Bernardo.

Side by side stand the witch-
hatted doll houses with their
awnings, wire fences, doily
lawns, grey-haired owners,
people from China, Russia,
Cape Breton, Orange Toronto.
Bums stuck on plastic porch
chairs, near-sighted eyes
investigate passing cars all the
cloudless, starless days and
nights on the eastern edge.

Three blocks south the Lake's
edge and *Corpus Christi*

where Bill Kurelek's sailor
feeds masses fish at picnic tables,
where our sons swim at a rooftop
pool and wander away
to the beach until a dwarfish man
seeing it happen
shouts and shakes his cane at us.
We are happy, welcomed
on our first Sunday,

by the church people
who shadow our lawn,
shout prayers for eternal
lives, then decamp silently.
We giggle with full mouths,
high on the good wishes of
strangers, the glory of owning
a Depression-era house
with its porches and panels,
the pride of meaningful work
and spirited offspring.

Our small place
that we give up,
we lose.

Saint John

My birth hospital
a burial mound
crowned by a brass dome.
Below, a beating maze
of freeways stretch over
the razed North end.
A traffic island erases
the sight of Grandpa's
Victorian pharmacy.
I'm the last of my tribe
in this city of hard heads
and busy bodies, citizens
who scatter generously
along rivers and sea,
loyal to the port
and its monuments
in Loyalist cemeteries.

For Sale our homestead in
the uneasily mixed South end.
A flat-topped, black-rimmed,
brick Victrola
of a Mecklenburg mansion,
built in shipping days
when men made money fast,
lost it quick to drink.
But Temperance-League Grandpa
dragged his brothers
out of ditches,
flew his children
to "higher callings"
in medicine and ministry.

In this city Aunt Dory
worked all her life for Sun Life.
Lyle race-skated to glory
on Lily Lake, painted
most of the town (brown).
Widowed Marion
bossed his brothers in business
until she lost her mind.
Uncle Bob bobbed away
to war in a corvette
on Courtenay Bay.
Teenage Mom prowled lonely
as the pulpmill clouds
over Reversing Falls,
after study with local masters
of Social Realism.
And I, fat with memory,
with longing,
have settled
into this rocky paradise,
secretive
as a black-painted house,
white lace curtains drawn.

The River People

The people we didn't know.
Mr. Bell's chipped farmhouse
high on the point's curve,
put in its place
by our tall hedges.
His rusted truck
flattened long grass,
chickens dressed
in the dust of the drive:
wild, smelly things
uselessly tried to claw
their way down.
Mr. Bell, the stuttering bachelor
fixed our summer houses,
mowed our lawns.
I was a child
wanting to play a princess
but I couldn't prance or preen,
just watch him work hard
with my head held low.

At 50 I live
on the Saint John River.
In summer I drive
to Brandy Point and peek
at the polished
Edwardian clapboards
and new mansions built
by new power brokers.
I pass by
Mr. Bell's resurfaced house
where a van stands

on the tar driveway.
I live downstream
on another point
with the river people,
the ones my parents
and I didn't know.
Though they keep a distance,
I overhear chat
about spoiled children,
renovations and acquisitions.

Wife: Glosa

> *And I will wear what dresses I choose!*
> *And I will dance, and what's to lose!*
> *I'm free of you, you little prick,*
> *And I'm the one to make it stick.*

> — Robert Creeley, "Ballad of the Despairing
> Husband"

On meeting her he says:
"Can't tell if you look good or not."
Tricky Dicky turns her head,
leads her dazed to bed.
She rises dazzled, dressed anew.
In gold and glossy mousse
she promenades herself and him,
and with foolish heart askew
cries: "Love has let me loose
"And I will wear what dresses I choose!"

The disco ball twirls and he says:
"Don't like dancing or this bizarre noise."
She turns down other beaus' requests
and gulps more tequila sunrise
than guts can stand until she spies
him *bumping* with a hopeful *cooze.*
Pumped up with still more booze
she knocks him down then drags him home
knowing she will always lose:
"And I will dance, and what's to lose!"

First time he leaves he says:
"We're like that old song *Wasted Days.*"

Flies North to ski with latest lay,
returns in spring with battered case.
Pleads at length his weary case,
works hard to comfort with his dick,
and as they stick themselves together
in a variety of oriental poses,
she tells herself: "With you I'll stick
until *I'm free of you, you little prick.*"

Two sons, one dies, and he leaves:
"I'm going through another phase."
Taxied home from maternity ward
she jumps into her small boy's arms.
Sitting son on wounded lap,
kissing him, she's free of Dick
and all the crap that held her back.
"Wanting Dick has made me sick.
With love at last I'll leave the prick.
And I'm the one to make it stick."

Punished for Life

The button-down
high-school boy
on TV who turns
into a shaggy dog.
A mutinous sailor
cat-of-nine-tails lashed
40 times in Technicolor.
Classmates' crippled
red hands after strappings.
Susan Hayward gas chamber
choked in "I Want to Live!"
14-year-old Stephen Truscott
on New Year's Eve
waits for his date
with the hangman.
Bernie C. called "Dirty Jew,"
kicked all the way home.
Roy John the girl-boy
and his bouquet
of fresh yellow
bruises each morning.
Your best friend locked
in the closet,
then taken
to the bedroom
by her "loving" Dad.
Yourself, emaciated giant,
loathed brainiac,
chased into corners,
thumped, threatened.
Yourself trying to execute
yourself –
slashes, pills, a drowning ...

The Marriage Ghost

I.

Gone the chameleon.
Gone my husband
who lives on,
with bejewelled Lady
(a divorcee like
the stoned cafe pumpkins
in Palma who had
intrigued my teenage self).

I first saw Lady
at my husband's health club.
Dainty ankles that bobbed
on limey suds, hooded eyes stuck
on my towelled man.
Then she snuck
into my night dreams:

Lady in Jaguar
screeches up to Signal Hill
Tower. Above fortress walls
she locks scrawny arms
round my husband's neck,
screams:
"What's mine is yours, darling."

I woke up on the King-Koil
mattress bought with long-gone
wedding monies, knew the ghost
would take our last breath.
So I embraced the space
between him and me.
No more vows, I vowed.

2.

All the women
our marriage ghost assumed —
Carol of the sighs,
Cossack-dancing Anya,
hunchbacked Tammy,
hysterical Laura Lee
and many more —
oh I do go on!

Then our ghost seized
my husband's form:
he watched himself
in the mirrors of our haunt
The Corona,
ripped up schnitzel as if
a ravening wolf
had won his hard-luck soul ...

Long ago ...
nowhere to go ...
A three ring circus,
Bar room door.

Her Daily Special

He calls himself my Ex.
Express train out of town.
Express elevator down.
Go away, Mr. X.

Leave me to my evening meal
at the Heavenly Divorce Cafe.
I'll have the usual
jack hot tamales.

Mineral water cleans me out,
cappuccino keeps me up,
a little absinthe down
in the Oblivion Room,

where I join divorcees
engaged in the gavotte, or perhaps
the garrotte? We form a conga line
of kicks to risible asses,

make out like bees, buzz
through to the bones
of our marriage beasts,
then toast to love deceased.

Dreams about Babies and Birds

I.

This time Baby is the size
and shape of a punching bag
(like the Popeye my sister
and I laughingly socked,
expelling the bad breath
of high-school afternoons).
Baby has the flowery scarfed
face of those wooden dolls
that fit one over each. I say:
"This girl can't breathe!"
Yet she smiles in my arms,
holds my eyes.

2.

Six years old I take home
a trembling green budgie
in a fries carton cave,
call him Jim. His new home
a steel cage my mother buys
at Eaton's. I fill seed buckets,
change paper rugs, cheer on
my flip-flapping boy
until I greedily get blue-violet
Sue who pecks Jim blind.
In fits of silent rage
I starve Sue,
preside over her rounds
of ebbing life,
her flops on pee-soaked,
turd-studded papers.

3.

My own children gone
from their mother's nest;
one bathed and dressed,
animated, strong in flight;
the other
a crackling cage of sores.

The Heirs of Ethel Rosenberg

(Inspired by the film Heir to an Execution *made by Ethel's grand-daughter Ivy Meeropol)*

From her nest
on the Lower East side:
Taken.
July 1950,
middle of the century's middle.
A spy without a code name.
Her little brother her accuser.

Life magazine's centrepiece,
Wan wife with dishpan hands.
Julius loves Ethel,
Mommy loves Poppy,
Two smiling sons,
each in cap and plaid jacket.

Ethel's powdered face
and curled hair
gloved in black.
Electricity burns
down the veins
of the soprano
who sang solos in synagogue.

Two lost boys
wired to the Dodgers.

Names and stories change.
The boys say:
"Why did she leave us?"

One son's daughter goes
where none have gone,
to Rosenbergs lost
all over America.
To Ethel's brother's house,
high-walled and blacked-out
like a prison.
She reports in lilting tones,
dances on point
around the pain.

She grew up with
her mother's love.

Tigers

After I saw the light
and flew through the gates,
I took a moment
to catch my breath,
and spy on all the friends
I had left behind.
All the beautiful girls and boys
torn to bits by tigers,
alive and begging
not to be, and as I thought
of the young who die alone,
the breath I had caught
grew and grew and grew,
into a roar,
and as I roared
I heard roars
from every edge of Heaven,
bright and loud and thrilling
like a thousand roller coasters,
a wildly militant
Mormon Tabernacle Choir

mimicking not
the sweet baby Jesus
of the Born-Again swanks
in their musty Cadillacs
stationed at the crosswalks
of a multitude of no-tell motels.
No, roaring like the Jesus son
of the Old Testament guy
when he threw out the money-
whores and championed
the sub-whores of the money-whores.
He who suffered the little children.

The Distant Self

He lay low in the drifting hull spitting bits
even gulls don't grab, when his little ship

hit a berg. A blueish lump of shedding skin
moving minutely south. With pick-axe he chopped

to the core, where his child self appeared
frozen in a silly grin, wanting all the world's love:

wastrel dull as a wave, maddening as a wet dog.
How glad he was to clear that icy bit of life

and head out of sight.

The Close Star

For all of us. All we have
to do is rise and set with you

and you are everywhere.
On our skin and in our blood,

you're a living relation and ancestor.
(The others known only in passing.)

You foretell nothing, keep no secrets,
give us everything you've got,

and after we've turned away,
you keep your deep, elegant distance,

ready when we're ready, to turn around
and receive you, in love all over again.

II.

SOME OF THE
WOMEN IN MY TREE

A Spoon Riverish Anthology

My Maternal Side

1. Mary Towne Easty (1634-1692)

I was born a Towne and a Blessing.
With my Goodwife sisters
Rebecca Nurse and Sarah Cloyce
victim of Salem craftiness.
Rebecca taken to the tree with me.
Sarah bailed out under a bale of hay.
58 years old, Bible in hand,
when I kissed my seven dear ones.
For the record:
"As affectionate as could be
expected when she departed."

Little Miss Lewis had pointed
her finger at me.
Claimed affliction at my hands.
How could my hands
be anything but clenched?
For I was not part of the Body
Politic. The first court acquitted
me and home I went for two days
until, dressed in slaves' chains,
I was brought back for *accounting.*
I begged my yawning judges
not to shed innocent blood:

I can say before Christ
Jesus I am free.
I have no complyance
with Satan in this.
I will say it, if was my last time,
I am clear of this sin.

Lies could have saved my corporeal
body but I had to keep safe
my eternal soul.
In 1711 final *accounting*:
twenty pounds of family compensation
for my "wrongful execution".

2. *Frances Everett Brown (1869-1952)*

My beauty was of no interest to me,
nor my husband's to him.
Clinton a distant cousin,
one I knew from earliest days.
We grew in prayer and ambition.
Two blue-eyed daughters and our
brown-eyed boy, Bliss.
Marion sent to Boston, Margaret
and Bliss to Nova Scotia
for their higher callings.
Scholarly Marion our pride
until she married
an unclean man.
Naturally we wore black
to the wedding.
Margaret with us always,
pure, unkissed.
Then Marion came back
home with her own two girls and boy.
The Grand Tour and our drift down
the Rhine: Not a patch on the Saint John River!
Gardening at Brandy Point,
windowed geraniums at Mecklenberg.
Snow-white lace,
no matter the coal.
I laced the boots
of the Temperance League.
Steamed sweet molasses
brown bread for Baptist Bazaars.
After Clinton died I grew sharp-tempered.
Made Marion cry and wonder
if I'd always felt that way about her.
Left behind well-disciplined,
Godly children and grandchildren.

3. Marion Brown MacGowan (1901-1963)

My father built us a winter palace in town,
a summer tower on the river.
We never thought about how
happy we were.
Mother baked the best bread and tortes,
Father drove us to the Point,
Mrs. Simpson cleaned
to Mother's high standards.
My father loved my intelligence,
laughed when I told him jokes in Greek,
smiled when I recited Byron and Keats.
Margaret and I camped with the Guides,
sang hymns at beach bonfires.
I went away to Baptist Acadia
for Classics, Boston for Business.
Father and Mother wanted me with them
always, but I met Lyle.
Three children later, he died,
and I took up Business, moved home.
Fired my lazy brother-in-law, operated
my husband's company productively.
My daughters so beautiful
I thought the stork must have brought them.
My son my soul. They all flew away
and I settled down to my summer tower,
a flat on Germaine, bridge with spinster friends.
My daughters a worry.
How could such perfection
not find perfection? Then a time came
when I had to live for myself.
Leave my worries behind.

4. Ruth MacGowan Fraser (1930-)

I grew up with too many people in the house,
escape from Saint John
my first ambition.
Bicycle marathons across town,
double features at The Capitol,
canoe trips down the river,
shakes at the Riv, Impressionism at the Voc,
flashlit maps and plans drawn
beside my pincurled, sleeping sister.
I wanted my widowed mother to myself.
No delinquencies unnerved her.
From 17 a traveller until at 21 went broke in Rome.
I might have been a doctor's wife in Rothesay.
But I chose Red, war vet and sportsman
full of wild joy. We wed in the Rockies,
settled on the Pacific. Lived in a wigwam
where I learned Haida women's secrets.
Two girls were born and I loved them
according to Dr. Spock.
My husband left the dams and quarries,
contained and marketed the life in him,
and made a good living.
I tried teaching, then stayed inside my house.
I have a talent for nursing and cared for Him
and my aunts until they died.
At 55 I got me to myself.
My neighbours spy on me, but I get my revenge.
I keep busy with new movies and the news.
With good wine and smokes
and a southern exposure, living is bearable.

5. *Patricia Fraser (1958-)*

High foreheads tight with tension.
Mother and Sister
walked out their fears
in each childhood house and year.
Dad whistled, called me out for spins.
But I couldn't listen
to his arias and false hopes.
Give me pop and paints, shovels and rakes,
freedom from those old funhouse mirrors.
Built my dollies castles,
designed Barbie's dresses.
School fortune teller,
girls' club Treasurer.
In high school flew away
with Biker Mike.
Came back down
and left him for Art College.
25 years with my Prince
turned toad until I ran off
with my true loves, my children,
deep and shining.
My Waverley Lakes windy willow cottage
bursts with oils, buckets, pots, balls, dogs,
and friends crashing wherever, whenever.
I've made peace with shadows.
Built my home in the light.

My Paternal Side

1. Georgina (Georgie) MacDonald Fraser (1862-1950)

Two MacDonald sisters,
two Fraser brothers.
Barbara and I strong young
Highland girls, six feet.
David and George old bachelors,
elders at the Kirk.
George had worked his way
up from the coal pits
to a mine office in Pictou.
Bought me a carriage house.
Two boys, three girls,
ginger-haired, straight and tall.
After George died I sold up
and took them to Montreal
so that they could be ladies
and gentlemen of McGill.
Pretty Mary sailed to Long Island
with Ernest the Pugilist.
Bill worked the continent
with Irene and their five scamps.
Constance and Jeffrey
painted in bohemian obscurity.
Princely Blair climbed to the top
of Mount Royal (Hotel).
Sturdy Clarice watered and weeded
the family gardens.
I grew fond of Bill's five,
charming, fast, mysterious.
I died surrounded by my family,
for whom God made me.

2. Clarice Fraser (1905-1996)

My family loved me so much
I had to be good.
When Father died, a girl threw herself
on his coffin crying:
"I love you, Mr. Fraser."
My sisters and brothers my best friends.
McGill and work with stuttering
brains at the Neurological.
I say you love the work you find,
not find what you love ...
My brother Bill a Captain
of hockey, football, Industry.
I matched him up with sorority girls,
but he stammered.
He fell hard for a wily dancer
down in the Ottawa Valley.
Hard work and hard drinking followed.
Many nights he came to me
chattering and sobbing.
I was rescued from a TB death
by my medical admirers.
Tiresome rest and the watery air
of Lake Placid where Norman Bethune
led pitiful rebellions and tried
to make love to me and take me to Mexico.
For thirty years I loved my married boss
in silence and almost died
again when he went by his own hand.
Nursed my beloved's wife and my mother.
Rich by inheritance
I brought myself back to Nova Scotia.

3. *Irenee Bedard Fraser Walker (1897-1992)*

French and Cree, *sans* Reservations.
Père *avec* lover skipped town,
Mère died by fire.
The nuns put me to work at ten.
I said I was a princess
lying in wait for my fortune.
At sixteen I joined a chorus line,
learned the Can-Can.
Men loved my hips
and sway and dainty feet.
A McGill college boy wanted to be seduced
so I complied.
He wed me with Irene coming,
and signed up for war.
The war ended too soon
and four more were born.
Bill made me quit French
and my homemade potions,
my rainy voice dried up
singing Presbyterian hymns.
No dancing except when I stepped out,
Bill away building bridges, highways.
Daughters born with my body
and Mary Fraser's face
easily married well.
My heartstopping son.
Bill willed his death at 65.
I thought I should die too,
but my children told me not to.
I took up painting.
My last husband a Glace Bay fiddler,
ten years younger but he went first.
I passed away in the Poor House,
singing French lullabies.

4. Irene Fraser Cunningham (1918-2005)

Grandma and Aunt Clarice
petted my baby self.
My parents returned but the other
mothers' love stayed with me.
We children fought
but I was Number One.
In the twenties we lived on Mount Royal,
bossed servants.
In the thirties Dad scrubbed our floors,
made soup and bread.
I was revered by the straight-up Frasers,
the hard-scrabble Bedards.
Queen of the Apple Blossom Festival.
While a nursing sister, set my cap
for Commander John, who left
his fiancée, married me *toute de suite.*
Converted for John
but not mystical like my mother.
Four children raised to do good and have fun.
John and I got sick and while I moaned,
he slipped away.
I ran John's store, loved gold,
damask and Baroque.
Free time at Neil's Harbour
watching for sea signs.
Painted Cape Breton with a talent like Mom's.
Died by centimetres,
my children trying to be patient.

III.

BOYS AND MEN

The Golfers

Haddie Morash, Bev Hamm,
Baldy Purdy, Big Red.
Winks, squints, grins, pats.
Capped sunburnt swingers in Raybans
and logo polyester salute the camera,
hurry stilted and super 8 fast
to the wide verandah
of the white-columned clubhouse
and pass through the black hole
of the open doorway.
In the next shot they've resurfaced,
bathed and brushed.
They slump in varnished captain's
chairs, raise toasts, down
icy Schooners and Exports.
In the purple twilight watch
a lone buddy, Douggy Doyle,
sink his putt.
Douggy tips his cap,
humbly lifts his burden of a bag
and heads to the pro shop.
There is a silent round of applause,
silent buying of rounds.

Not that she knows much.
One night her father's golfer friends appear.
Her mom zooms off to a movie.
She sits at the top of the stairs, hears brag
of fuckable women and the others,
"The Bow Wows". She has freckles,
glasses, cropped hair.
Creeps to her room, glad of the muffle.

They've *vamoosed, skedaddled,*
by the time her mother returns
and finds the water marks,
the butts, the burns and ashes.

Tall Tales

I picture him in the War,
with his Scottish ancestors,
on an Orkney island hilltop,
telling stories that stretch
into the racing clouds
that carry them west to Ireland
where they grow taller.

My father enters a hospitality suite
full of dull farts
comparing stocks and golf scores,
parts the way and makes them
snort and chortle,
think themselves witty and jolly.
All eyes on my father's
slits of glee,
his throat guzzles golden suds.
The shake of the head.
Isn't it all crazy
and wonderful?

Childhood tales for his children:
yodelling in Tennessee,
his father's golf game with mobsters
in Louisville,
his mother who dies and comes back
at a public pool in Lexington.
How he wins the tri-State tennis trophy,
then moves back to Nova Scotia
where he's beaten up for playing tennis
and becomes a hockey star.
That we shouldn't care about bullies.

Dare them to punch us as he did
after secretly boxing.

When I was a young woman deadlocked
in grief over my faithless husband,
he told me about his red-haired golfer
true love who married and divorced
four times,
and the cheerful nurse who wore his ring
all through the War, then left him
for a frat boy,
and my beautiful mother who broke his heart
on the honeymoon.
Said I should give up what's not mine.

My father, who in his morphine-addicted dying,
told stories to a pot of geraniums
he thought was a hospital visitor,
traded tales in French with his senile mother,
whispered jokes after swigs of lemon barley.
The force who fought death
with each gasp left,
to tell his story.

Two Triolets for Grandpa

I. The Queenston House

I stop at the river front house
where I lived as a girl of four
with Grandpa Moose and Grandma Mouse,
a stucco Art deco house
full of oils and crafts by Grandma Mouse.
Grandma stoic in silks and pearls
stood tall when drunken Grandpa hurled
himself around that pretty house.

2. Heart Attack

The Midwest winds blew low and wide,
grey river banks filled up with snow,
the day Grandpa stomped out and died.
Some rye and pills helped ease the ride
enough to shovel until he died.
The fat man's heart prepared to go,
a blood-red face adrift in snow.
The winds blow low, the winds blow wide.

Father and Son

My son was born the morning after my father died.
The day before the Montreal Massacre.

All week Mom lit candles for the souls of dead girls.
I cried in my bed until the Demerol arrived.

Then limped down four stories to see
the twelve-pound linebacker in his suit of boiled skin.

The baby with his grandpa's deep-set watchful eyes
that measure the playing field, prepare the game.

And I thought they could have met in passing,
one carried from coma, one heave-hoed to breath ...

My son's long sleep through homecoming, then the
wake up red-alert. The smallest sound, the softest touch.

How We All Start

Who says he has to come out of me like me?

"His bones are small" my big-boned mother says.
So muscular his legs bow, limbs curl into torso.
So long and skinny he seems to be losing weight.
But the doctor declares him a fine big lad.
He's rough with my nipples, guzzles for hours,
wriggles in my arms, Nijinsky leaps
in his Jolly Jumper clear across our scuffed floor.
Like his wiry father a hard one to pin down.

But there, see, my own fierce expression pierces me.
My own freckled pink skin tender to the touch.
Myself, who after waking studies the room's world
long and discerningly before crying out for company.

Missing Boys

The NICU nurse shook her head
at my younger son. Said:
"I'm not holding out hope for this kid".
I thought, you slut, his blood sugars are good,
he's the most beautiful baby on the unit.
There's something missing,
she'd been dying to lay on me.
I held the bunting bundle and knew it too.
But he was mine, had been wrenched out of me.
(A brain "globally delayed" by hospital drugs?)
A future of shocking diagnoses
by nurses, doctors, teachers.
My desire to punch them
ratcheted up the pain in my gut.

My older son had suffered a ventilator, more drugs,
eleven days in a wiry, cramped cage.
Yet the beet-faced kicker tired out his nurses.
"This kid is high maintenance" one said.
And he grew into a tiny whiny rabble-rouser
threatened by circus guards
when he tried to jump out of rides ...
But after cruel come-uppances
The Power King vanished;
no more "I'm so a cited!"
A quiet teenager learned the *right moves*;
home movies the only evidence
that other boy existed.

My younger son, enraged by the world
and his brother,
did the unbearable:

he and his guitar left home, ran.
A Saint John Police investigation,
and I was grilled, taped, my son's room
dusted for prints and blood spatter,
until a lady called the cops and said the boy
was down at the old refinery smoking weed
with a strange young man.
More escapes until he was rounded up in cuffs,
a guest of the jail before taken to the psych ward
where it took weeks for him to recognize me.
When he came home from that lost and found,
his older brother had found asylum,
then went off to college these past four years.
My younger son is at home in his way,
my missing, ever-present boy.

Fire

A boy jumped into a beach bonfire
on a hunting trip with Poppy and the lads.
Poppy carried the boy on his back
to a helicopter
that flew three hundred miles
so the boy could stay alive
and wear a plastic mask
and lurch
like a little Frankenstein monster.

A boy stopped eating.
A tube was shoved down his throat
so vitaminized condensed milk
could course through his stalk of a body.
Trays of food thrown at him
untouched.
Face like Kleenex
stretched over sticks,
eyes round as marbles.

Two untouchables,
uselessly loved,
parents nursing their own wounds.
Then, the boys opened their doors
and sadness flew away.
The boys played
and ate, ate and played,
laughter raging through their small beings
like fireflies, like shooting stars,
lighting their way.

Lazy Days at the Psych Ward

Frank asks the doctor to cut his head off.
Jurgo back from his mission in Palestine.
Twittering Bob hoots and darts.

These are my son's mates now he's sixteen
and supposed to be an adult.
My slumped boy appears not to notice them,
eyeballs *Judge Judy* then *King of the Hill.*
But they continue to tell him to try
to eat the disgusting food, put on underwear,
comb his chopped-up hair.
One says: "All you need is good weed."

Last year my son was strapped down by cops,
sirened away to join boys
who set fires, jump off roofs, expose themselves.
My son livened up there, hugged his toys.
Playing dumb, he was sent home again
to torture his mind, slowly starve.

Perhaps my son will let the man in him be known.
Please God he will go on.
And if he's back here telling professionals
there's nothing wrong with him,
he needs to go home to protect his mom,
I'll be glad of his patient mates.
Naked, proud, *thoughtful.*

Psychiatrist's Notes on Boy

Exultations to examinations!
We all know
the unexamined life's
not worth living.
Let's study his mother's lamentations,
his social workers' procrastinations,
his daily mastications.
After diagnosis prognosis,
rotations notations.
Pills prevent invention.
Thought follows ought.
Good should.
Blame him, shame him,
let the stinky little bear bare his soul
and bear it all.
Inured to shock he won't talk back.
Don't balk boy, go back boy,
to your water and boob tubes.
I wanted Magic, Boy.
Wha Wha Ooosh!
I've seen enough from you.
There's no hope so make do.
Haste makes waste.
Next case.

The Game

Coming home he flies down Clark Road
past the cul-de-sac sign
into the blue on blue
on his way into Grand Bay;
the rollovers, the splashes,
like held breath,
an outage.

At twilight he hits the inland highway
and the perfect antlered moose
squashes his car
like a pop can.

Those blurry winter evenings
when what he wants to do is snowplow
into the ditch
and never wake.

The police come to his door
to tell him that his son
walked toward the five pm train,
Laid his body down
on the track
and waited.

JANET FRASER

Moose

On the lam from Newfoundland, fat with joy,
I sold my mouldy house, divorced Dr. Chaos,
quit the worst job known to humankind.
Now I'm a manic, Maritime tourist
renting a Saint John River shack,
surrounded by critters, crows, car parts.

My son and I lie in on weekends,
he in a dark locked room with Stephen King,
me tossing on a dry, hard bed,
until one windless morning we take a ride
to New River Beach and the low tide.
Then my boy whispers:

"Keep on keeping on. Go, Mom, Go."
So I drive, past the Pennfield blueberry fields
down the Fundy shore to Chocolate Town,
sluggishly line dance across the border,
tour Calais' shabby treasures,
and he says: "On to see Stephen King's house!"

I settle on a plywood cell in a Bangor motel;
wet setters shake their fur by the slimy pool.
Then we're off to see gargoyles, bat gates,
and Jeeps indicating the gore meister's home.
Quick stop for toothpaste in this foreign place.
Long night when my son snores louder than the TV.

Next day, July 17. No gift on my special day.
No person willing to sing me the silly song.
But glad enough I speed along the Airline road
when straight out of woods into noon-hour sun

76

a ghastly golden horse crosses the barrens –
I swerve left and floor it and close my eyes.

Then open them expecting the wild patch
we roll into is Heaven, before realizing
it's plain Maine weeds and plain mother
and son, perfectly alive ...
My half-assed wreck feels like a toy truck
as I exultantly return to the land of my birth.

Manning up to It

She's a woman with no wish to be a man,
yet has been taken for one.
She fears men who want to be women
when they're six feet and broad like her.

She imagines a male life.

Instead of compliments for white curls
and cornflower eyes,
adults notice how well he speaks,
how beautifully he runs and swims.
He's a strong, smart boy,
not an older, big-boned girl,
one not laughed at for playing
Cinderella in the school's French play;
his Prince Charmant a *real charmer*.

A tall muscular teenager,
he dates those he wants,
not anyone who asks. The college swim star
has places to go, not a lonely walk back
to residence room after races.

The middle-aged male poet who
enlivens sensitive minds, never
enrages the untalented.

Best of all he tells his loves he loves.
Tells all of the cold sex-crazed losers to get lost.

Trust/Tryst

(In memory of Dr. David Craig)

He seemed second-rate,
prone to lectures and warnings.
His office raggedy, clients poor.
He wagged a beefy finger,
his black eyes glowed,
the embers at the end of a Presbyterian sermon.
"What kind of working woman with teens
to support puts garbage in her mouth
knowing she's diabetic?"

The funny thing is I passed out on him,
my first coma.
Epileptic on his bed at noon
when he needed food and smokes.
He was gentler after that,
until a crisis with my second-born.
Once done, he himself was rushed
to hospital for surgery.
Typical doctor, it was said,
doesn't take care of himself.

Wanting the usual uppers and downers
next time I saw him,
I noticed he had gained weight,
seemed distracted, his hands shook,
though he still liked to pat my bum.
(And flushed when I flirted
and praised his dedication.)

One day I snuck my file
and found out that my visits
amounted to "Depression, Depression,
Depression, Depression".
I wasn't angry because I'm one of those broads
who craves a doctor's attention and affection.
Only found out he had died
after I went to my appointment.
In shock I was taken care of by his younger,
better-looking brother
who glanced at my history, prescribed nerve pills.
I didn't have the energy
to start up my sob stories nor the will,
scared that I had helped finish Dr. David off,
but knew it wasn't true,
because he was a man who liked attention
even more than I (do).

Strap Across the Back

I.

It's you at the wheel of the electric blue
convertible, mother and daughter act in back.
That Victory sign, the smooth way you roll in
to the station car park. Thick black waves,
bony body gone by the roadside.
Twenty years on, your eyes swallowed up
by puddled cheeks, chest sunk into belly,
long thin strands almost white.

2.

Ghost to you now, I was shadow when we met.
Then, grinding together under dancehall lights,
you smiled. *Bella Baby*, you said,
twirled me round like a lasso,
and I never flew higher except inside you
in banged-up motel rooms. You talked big about
taking me down, but my lust was just
as great, watching the flash of black and blue
in that cowboy saloon's flecked mirrors.

3.

Life began on Lennox Island with grandpa,
the marathoner. As a lad he looked like you
in suspenders on a 1912 Herald page:
"Will The Great Red Man Win Again?"
Grandma sang and rocked you. Sent away
to the Shube school, you weren't told
that they died when their cabin burned down.

Children's Aid put you on a Greyhound
that crossed the border. Whoosh,
big doors opened to the Port Authority.
Last good moment before my life turned to shit.
In Washington heights blow, rape and whip.
Became your precinct's best runaway until
you spilled it in Court and the judge roared *Liar.*
Life sentences: reform, labour, war … moving always.

4.

I might have tried my own moves, held you
longer. All the I love You jive, and your bit
by bit dissolve. I agreed to join you skydiving
by the time you had disappeared.
No hard feelings old man, I was a soft touch.
Your sauntering strut, your jumpy long body
light on mine.

Hard of Hearing

Your pitch perfect, your black auk music devilishly good.
You married a concert player because you liked her hands.
Her silence. Wrote one another for years,
divorced. Lovers got you alone at first,

and you told the tale of the pale, fragile pianist
from another city. I read about your true first love
in your obituary. An Irish girl who sang at your father's
saloons.
Said she was going places, but went only to bars

in small-town Wisconsin. You ran away from her in Chicago
at the State Fair. Thought you could see the world if you hid
in the stockyards with the bulls waiting to be butchered.
Once found Mom's belt branded your hide.

Then, on the back stoop, behind the blood sausages
Mama pinned you with knife to throat, nicked
you like a painter nicks a bubble. Perhaps
brain and heart disconnected then. I used to long

for your winks, the dusky voice. A courtship of wine, song
and flattery. But you flirted too long with a biker girl. And
after all the kisses it was no good. The death notice noticed
you came from Winomee Falls. Winomee Falls makes me
think

of animated bluebirds, Disney overtures. Bluebirds of giddy joy,
"One more for the road." Your bull head steamed with vodka,
a knife at your throat as you flew beltless through dawn sleet
into a ditch. We heard you.

The Missionary's Son

Born half-way between China and England
you were given Canadian citizenship,
something that came in handy.

Too clever for the parsonage
you won places at Eton and Cambridge,
acquired the right brand.

You wooed a sunny lady of Gibraltar
away from the hushed Moorish world
you loved so well.

Exchanged continents for a maritime college,
where among the apple trees
you perfected magical seductions.

Then you kissed the Town Burgher's wife
and made the burgher cry.
(A marriage saved by Palm Beach.)

Sans famille you skittled off to a new town,
secretly bamboozled a teenager's heart,
settled for suitable pursuits.

Retired, you live high in forested hills
above river flood plains, with feeders, Jeeps
and a sporty girl companion.

In winter you dive on the coral reefs
of a Third World country, study Mayan ruins
and trade washed-up little treasures.

I saw you at a fall market once, blond hair now
a grey tail the length of your back. Closed lips
smiling you passed me by, stiff as a dog collar.

Bait and Tackle

"I *am* Michael!" I shout to the Nerepis marsh.
Think of *my* Heathcliff, seven feet,
tromping in Wellies the barrens of Paradise,
silver hair waving.

Astride my boat I toast Mike
with a stone mug like the red Trouty beach
rocks he warmed. I held the long, wide hands
that rubbed them smooth.

My glasses frame the glinting marsh grasses,
sharpen the shore's edge, like the pale fire
of Mike's squinting eyes
when he steered his course to Topsail Bay.

Luminous bass, big soul man that got clean away.
(Tossed out the bait, overlooked the hook.)
Can't keep what's not caught.
The rest of it stays, close to the vest.

Things I Loved

Your high office windows on mauzy days,
the long arms that hooked them open and shut.
Your Mustang we rode in to a Tim's,
the bucket seat where I left literary films
for your wife, rushed to my husband's car.

Seal Cove Carnival and our drive to an arena.
Your black size 14 hockey skates that flew you
grinning round and past me.
Your lumbering shoulders, endless legs.
Your honking drawl: *"Catch if catch can."*

Your A-Frame shack with the emerald roof
that ruined sleep the summer of skylights.
The blue-gold kitchen we sat in after a conference
so I could phone home to my children
and dawdle over cups of tea, longing to stay ...

Now I wonder, did you listen to my Tom Rush CD?
Read the poetry books I gave you?
Watch the sad movies your wife and I collected?

Occupations: A Picaresque

El profesor's loving tongue
smothers her objections.

A tight-lipped drummer
snares her with tippy arms.

Housemate a rumpled old shirt
that never fits quite right.

A blind date moves in to her
so fast and happily she just laughs.

Monsieur Ennui wears her out
like that weary song *Je t'aime.*

Taking her on board an Athenian rower
raises his oar and shoves off.

Her pilot flies them out of town
one starry summer night.

A rover tracks her down
whistling west to his sea shanty.

A prowling Stingray salesman
pokes her bucket seat backside.

Her leading man plays both priest
and thug in a long-running show.

Her hefty chef whose beefsteak
sizzle flashes in the pan.

The war vet hands out pleasure and pain
as if the same − *pathei mathos.*

She meets her captain on a crossing
tossing them over in salty heat.

She falls for a tall man's tales and dreams
waking to find him long gone.

Lifting her high on his puffy shoulders
the body builder pumps up her silly smile.

Windswept at Yonge and Bloor

(after reading Lorca)

The wind's a gallant
blowing greenly round her stems.
Horned Pan, satyr of these city corners,
smiling asks her to dine with him,
leaning parts the crowd and leads her on.
He's come down from the mountains,
she's travelled west from the ocean.
A strongman from way back,
he could lift her high on his shoulders,
carry her away to the Inn,
which he will,
in his own time.
Some fear the northern night wind,
the night dew, the moonlight.
But the wind woos her gently,
before showing her the wrath of
Boreas.
Too late for calls of alarm
she is taken
by his fury,
trembles at his seizures.
The dark-maned stallion mantles her,
the sleepless wind wraps her round,
holds her tight
until he's ready to ride off.

IV.

SELF-PORTRAIT

Self-Portrait

1

Banished
from my home,
naked to the world
and lacking cunning,
I let them turn me
on to my backside.
Like a pelt of water
shiftlessness clings.

2

Pilgrim wandering
from Paradise
to Bare Need,
I'm on my lonely, Sir.
Come over here,
kiss me rough.
Take me to your room
in the grotto.

3

Like silver plate
I wear out in the light.
A kingdom of fossils
made for me.
Can be probed,
but gently.
In harmony
a leading note.

4

Wrong-headed
when wronged.
Brought up with girls.
Pulled into the wave,
a crash of impulses.
A love zombie,
will broken
by longing.

The One Who Stays

> *There are always, in each of us,*
> *Those two: the one who stays,*
> *The one who goes away —*
>
> — Eleanor Wilner

I am the one
who stays.

I said no
to nursery school.
Clung to Mommy's knees,
did not let her pry away my hands.
Stayed by her side
in our apartment with the
bamboo blinds and view
of Lombardi poplars.
Followed her to her bed
when my baby sister
fell asleep and held her limp
body in my pudgy arms.

I said no
to private girls' school.
Walked home for lunch,
ate Campbell's soup
with my mother,
caught the noon hour
gangster flick on TV
while she washed
diapers and sighed.
Sat on her lap
on the spongy sofa
and sang show tunes.

I said no to Big Cove
summer camp.
Read sexy books,
swam in public pools
with poor kids,
chased Dad's golf balls,
stayed late playing
handball until Mom
led me home
to our apple orchard
and a glass of creamy milk.

I said no
to college in a city far away.
Sauntered to university classes
with girls I knew from school,
played Varsity,
stayed average.
Caddied for Dad,
dated males
my own age, felt
safe and reasonably
comfortable in my skin.

I said no
to nervous breakdowns
and rested at home.
I said no to flying
to a remote location
where no one found me.
Said no
and spent time with
my father before he died,
became my sister's
best friend.

I am the one
who says no and stays.
No I am the one
who wanted to say
no I am the one
who always goes away.

Child's Play

What bothers me
is not Persephone half-time in Hades
or Icarus and his foolish flight.
It's the Centaur, trapped in a horse's flanks.
As a child watched *The Shaggy Dog*
and screamed at a boy growing claws and fur.
In college heard about women pumped
by Great Danes and wanted to commit
mass murder, then shoot myself.

At the Halifax Ladies College
bachelor teachers, and their resignation.
Noon bells chimed and we all
sat down at our appointed places.
Students, daughters of doctors and lawyers.
And loner girls with parents like my own,
crawling down in the world.

At home hissed at myself.
Hid in the attic room with the gouged walls
while parents fought.
Played giddy freaks with a girl sent down
to reform school. Ran away, picked up by cops.

My father's family choice spirits;
saw them rarely, in batches of carnival fun.
I wanted things both ways, but all I did was
mix it up and leave a blur
like an oil that's been painted over
so many times it's a blob.
Drone, useless daughter, unloved lover.

"It's our hot French blood," Daddy said.
Blood that burns along the nerves.

Best Friend

Early in life girls double up,
or compete in friendship love triangles.
I had a couple of sister twins
in my move-around childhood.
Then I zoomed in on The One,
although I didn't know why.
A diplomat's daughter,
she said "My word!" and "Oh golly!"
Classmates called her Tiny Tim,
her hair was that thin,
and she loved to sing shrilly.
She did a wicked Fagan,
twisting fingers, bulging eyes.
Yet she was an angel with her spun gold crown.
We wore tutus and danced Swan Lake
at the Conservatory,
learned lifesaving in the marvellous
subterranean green Y pool,
laid bluebells on pioneer graves,
tried out churches all over greater Halifax,
baked cakes and snuck Scotch
in her mother's apartment,
told the sad stories of our mothers' lives;
we wrote and illustrated a witchy book,
stalked handsome members of the Sociology Club,
played Maggie Smith
in The Prime of Miss Jean Brodie,
chased Peter Sellers around Manhattan
in The World of Henry Orient;
we hitched a ride on the Montreal train
but were stopped by the police in Windsor Junction;
at school's end we flew to Maine

and partied with her diplomat father,
who tried it on with each of us.

Away at different colleges, she met her husband
while I dated ill-suited boys and men.
Forty years on our lives touch at the edges,
and we say: "So glad I had a friend!"

First Lover

A duck à l'orange supper by candlelight.
Me in my lady-like dress and hose, nerves all a quiver.
Flamenco, Feliciano, Tom Rush,
troubadour poetry and his pale blue air-mail letters.
Long-stemmed red roses, a golden Cancer crab necklace
and his golden skin after a month in Malaga.
These things brought me closer and closer
but I pulled back,
wanting my chance with a boy,
not wanting my heart hurt.
He had told me he dreamt
I was his final lover, that he died by my side,
and I think he was my final lover too,
the one who seduced with love in his heart

Holiday

Me ma's on the lam
from the Mounties, the CIA, the neighbours.
We're in shifts, flip-flops, TCA flight bags
the wiggling stewardess gives us.

The free agent, cocktail in one hand,
cigarillo in the other, toasts our escape
to the skies with shaved buzzing men.

Then the tarmac prance, Mom's head high,
shoulders back. Bags swooped out
of the carousel, cab snapped up.

*

At midnight Mom rents
a four-seater and flies us off
storm-swept Jekyll Island down
to the hot spot on the map,
Miami Beach. We're safe
at the top of the Belle View tower,
the stalking white light a mere crack
in the Venetian blinds. Daily dips
in and out of the salt-water pool,
the effervescent blue so brilliant
my eyes hurt, and beyond, the sea
promises further escape.

*

Last year Sis and I frolicked in a French city,
swam in a blue Hilton circle,
decided which tucked-away lane

we'd choose for studios, the school
our children would attend.
Flying home we began brawling, then
stayed silent for a month until
we decided where we'd holiday next summer.

*

This year I spent a week with a man
from another continent inside a hotel room
and in a coffee shop where we befriended
tourists from Japan, Ukraine, Pakistan.
We hurtled around in subway cars,
laughed at our indirections,
promised forever at the airport. Back
at my cabin in the woods
I shout my sorrow to my pillow,
swear I'll never go away again.

Our Reunion

The landing strip marooned by fog and sudsy waves,
mid-Atlantic for all we know,
the jet's prosthetic arm leading us to a submarine ...

Instead, LaGuardia and the planet's city state.
We grab a cab, zoom across the East moat's bridge,
crawl by Trumped-up communes,

red flashes gracing the greyness. Midtown Marriott,
an abrupt twirl around a floodlit drive-in where
tipsy friends tip into one another's arms.

Then arm-in-arm along the Avenue we sashay,
stop at Grand Central for oysters
from Long Island, Cape Cod, Malpeque, Caraquet ...

MOMA, child's play with Klee and Pollock.
After *Starry Night*, done in by man-made Art
we strike out for the Park,

watch ducklings, dream of our Atlantic homes,
wake calls to sons who says *Yes, No, Sweet.*
Declare we'll take five males to Manhattan,

keep house on the East (or West) side ...
At the Tavern, dining on the Romantic Past,
our marriages, one lonely, one gone,

our children, breathing somewhere without us.
Morning shadows, mournful towers of suitcases.
Back to lives chosen, newly awkward

in skins that stretch to house old hungers.
Days ahead of any length and quality.
Friendship that holds fast or falls.

Mother Love Poem

Expecting my mother's Sunday evening call
I pick up the phone, and with all the good will
I can muster, bluster: "Mom! How are you?"
And my ex-husband, in a falsely flustered falsetto
flutters: "Lovely, lovey! Lovely!"

*

How lovingly I once regarded
Mom's large, coffee-coloured freckles.
How graceful she seemed in high-heel shoes
and the pastel linen dresses
Grandma's dressmaker mailed from Saint John.
Those exultant afternoons when the Queen
in rhinestone crown and satin cloak drank tea
and ate Easy-bake cake, in my cleaned-up bedroom.

*

How slow my mother's disappearance act.
The crazed, sad days without a glimpse of Mother.
Years on, her sudden reappearance in the night,
claiming escape from the clutches of CSIS.
Then the sneak and peek into every bit of my life
when I had children, as she tried to take them away ...
Mother madness, the gut-churning futility of it!
All of her concussions, tumbles, falls from grace
enough to kill the stately Queen Bee
and her charge. Yet the small, measured love
I feel for her, persists —

Don't Leave Me

Once my father and I took up church.
I refused to learn the catechism
and we began bowling.
Praying I've tried. When Dad died
God brought him bounding back
through my dreams. When my son
lost his mind and a Les Paul guitar
God assured me all would be well.

Hell! There's nobody there.
Wolves have souls too, and we don't
think about *their* trips to cloud or fire.
We're in love with our brains,
can't believe they waste like bulbs
or long-gone galaxies.

One murky day I drowned at Merrywood,
saw a light come and go
before waking to my auntie's breath.
Let body and soul stop together, I say.
Gracias a la vida. Carpe diem. And all that jazz.

Domestic Drama: Eight Prose Poems

I. Tic

When telling women friends about it, she recalled the four o'clock tugboat distantly upriver and me a sandy-assed two-year-old pointing to it with my wobbling arm, my fat old man's face quivering. "Go, go," I growled, my forehead furrowing like the boat's linear plow through eelgrassy tea. It got to be a regular thing with me and by the time I went to school kids stared repulsed when I let go, in bursts of scrunch and eye-glaze and lip-licks, the hot chills of my dreamworld's carnival thrill rides. So she took me to her psychoanalyst and smiling he spoke softly to my mother after she had paid the receptionist: "She's a normal girl reacting to the stresses of an abnormal home."

2. Lights Out

At night I tucked myself in, but not before I had laid all of my dollies round my pillow, a semi-circle of blind, dumb buddies. Pat Doll had a special place beside me, my only child, not like my baby sister Pat Real across the room, who turned her back. Like me Pat Doll's white hair was a tangled bush, her face and body covered with stains, a sore, fat tummy. Like my mother I didn't wash my face or brush my teeth at night, no longer knelt beside my bed because nobody cared about my dollies but me. I went out to play in my zipped sweater jacket and burred beige leotards until some women said I should wear a skirt over them. I told my mother and she kept me at home until spring when I wore my tartan skirts and sandals. My mother loved me, I was part of her, loved as she loved herself, turning off the bedroom light.

3. Spank

Two girls in matching pixie cuts and nautical jackets, the cute smirking one pointing a finger at her towering, cowering big frig of a sister, home from church, slamming the giant doors of Dad's smoothie Bel Air. In the vestibule, my sister says: "Come on, she needs her spanking," and after they, snickering, whisper together, I make my get-away; he grabs my ankles and belly flops me and pretend spanks me clapping his big hands together behind my bum. Then three years before he dies, diagnosed with cancer, not even 60, fired from his job and terminally sad, he asks me if I *do anything* as a librarian and not happy myself I say: "Well, I don't lose my jobs." And my father's spanking hand forms a tight fist, and he presses it hard into the dishwasher he's leaning against and in a tone I've not heard before, he says: "Is that so?"

4. Mouth

My aunt's lips were fat and pink, every bit as pretty as her bitty ears, blonde braided hair, full breasts, and her skirted swim suit. Her mouth was open most of the time babbling to her son and beautiful daughter, so she didn't notice me, who couldn't swim, walk off the lake's sandy shelf, though I had been warned. I dropped down so deep, so fast, my sculling arms couldn't break the lake's skin, water-blinded I couldn't discern their figures. As I blacked out I regretted my short foolish life and death. Next thing hot, sour breath pushed hard into my mouth, a mouth on mine, in and out, then I sputtered and opened my eyes and my aunt was inside me, outside me, her pretty lips bruised, her pretty body strong as Hercules when she lifted me up.

5. Falls

When I think of the poet (Robert B.) I saw at Union Station the day he took the train to Niagara Falls, the one whose wife had left him, the one whose body was pulled out of the river in spring, I think of my early childhood in a Niagara Falls apartment with my mother who kept kitchen clippings of mothers who killed their children, but I don't think of my trips with my ex to the Falls where I drank champagne on the Gardens balcony at dusk when the rainbow lights came on, yet I remember the teenager I was when I saw *Niagara* and cried myself silly over the poor schmuck set up for a water-logged fall by Marilyn Monroe and her lover, and I wondered if a woman's beauty and body language gave her not just the power, but the right, to kill, and did my father ever want rid of me too?

6. View

My father had a turkey neck that zinged this way and that, when he saw a pretty woman, bit of leg, tight sweater, in his V8 powered car driving me to lessons downtown. He took his family to the Ice Capades and shot all the Cadettes numbers, sequinned torsos, fish-netted thighs, over and over. He visited the hotel where the *girls* stayed and returned saying: "The pancake makeup covers pits, their teeth are false." He filmed my statuesque mother getting on and off planes so often people said: "Is she someone we may have heard of?" Dad boasted about his married sex life to houseguests, which mortified and bewildered me. My friends and I raided his drawers, read *Playboy*, *The Story of O*, *Police Story*. My parents cruised to Manhattan in the fall, where Dad filmed The Rockettes at Radio City.

7. The Mall

In Scarborough my life ground on from one spanking to the next. Always at the strip mall where grim Mom quick as shit pulled down my pants and smacked my puddle cheeks. At four I asked my mother not to spank me anymore, 'cause it hurt my feelings, and she stopped, making me promise to be good until we got home, when she could lock her bedroom door. I ran away from home to the Golden Mile mall where Mom found me on the mechanical pony trotting and begging passersby for dimes. On junior-high weeknights I took off smoking to the Halifax Shopping Centre where I sucked on hard candies and relaxed at the Eaton's makeup counters and teen magazine racks until nine when the lights were dimmed and all the mall rats bum-rushed into the night.

8. Dr. Fraser

My mother bought medical handbooks in order to treat her grave illnesses. She worked her way through them, starting with brain cancer. She diagnosed me a giantess and tried to shorten my legs with splints until Dad put a halt to sleepless nights. She saved money to fly me to Australia for hormone shots, but my father prevailed. Our family doctor, James Fraser, pulled out my toenail, allowed no tonic, and ripped off my forehead a purple pock. At 19 I kept my college rape a secret and boiling listened to him chastise me for contracting crabs. My father golfed every day, no early diagnosis, my mother blamed our doctor for his wasting away. Dad died at home, Mom shooting him up with morphine every four hours. At 80 Mom sustains herself with wine and ciggies and never gets sick, not even a cold.

Leaving Nova Scotia

"Ca-na-da! (One little, two little,
three Canadians) We-e love Thee!"

In Pointe Claire
on a hot silvery afternoon

you are waiting, kerchiefed
and paisley tent dressed,

in front of the tearfully
windowed Eaton's mannequins,

giant button-eyed Barbie
and Ken in pastel pantsuits,

for Aunt J., who will swerve, wave,
dash to your arms, kiss lip

and cheek, rush you
into your uncle's grilled Lincoln.

The groovy cool days of '67,
when you love your cousins' brand new

split-level, egg-shell painted house
where you run crazy over this flight

of shag carpet stairs and that flight
to the plywood rec room for wrestling

with two man-child devils,
then sit down to the red maple-leaved

TV tables laden with wieners, chips
and root beer, and go-go boots tapping

you invisibly frug along with Robbie Lane
and the Disciples on Music Hop.

Next morning a shimmering island
of geodesic dome, inter-galactic, inter-

active, international. Your first red wine cheesy
fondue at dusk, deep purple

evening holding all of that enervating swamp heat
inside you as you stumble

to the commuter train that tumbles you round
your seat and brings you

back fast and jittery to your blessed temporary
split-level sanctuary, where you are

safe inside the unfamiliar.

ACKNOWLEDGEMENTS

Variants of several of the poems in this collection have been published in *The Antigonish Review, The Dalhousie Review, Nashwaak Review, Riddle Fence* and *The Toronto Quarterly.*

I am grateful to Anne Compton and Robert Moore for sensitive readings of an early draft of many of the poems. Thank you to Karen Solie, Sue Sinclair, and John Barton for their enthusiasm and constructive criticism of late additions to the collection. Warm thanks to Patrick Warner for praise.

A big thank-you to Michael Mirolla, my editor, and to Guernica Editions for giving these poems a fine home.

ABOUT THE AUTHOR

Janet Fraser was born in her mother's ancestral home, Saint John, and returned over 40 years later. In the meantime she lived for long stretches in Halifax, Toronto, and St. John's. She earned an MLS and an MA degree in English Literature from the University of Toronto, then worked for many years at *The Globe and Mail*. Currently she works as a librarian for the University of New Brunswick, and hibernates on the Saint John River with her two sons. Her poetry has been widely published in journals and anthologies, and her first poetry collection *Long Girl Leaning into the Wind* was shortlisted for the Newfoundland and Labrador Book Award. She publishes fiction, memoir, and book reviews, and teaches part-time at UNB's College of Extended Learning.

PRAISE FOR THE AUTHOR'S
LONG GIRL LEANING INTO THE WIND

Janet Fraser's first collection of poetry is a feast of sensory detail, dream images, and fantastical visions — the whole amounting to a rich episodic autobiography.

— The Telegram

Whether a startling lyric image or an exploration of language and memory, each caught moment, each poem, is like a stone dropped in a lake ... surprising the reader on some far shore.

— Atlantic Books Today

Several pleasures await the readers of Janet Fraser's Long Girl Leaning into the Wind ... engaging reflections on life's changes and passages ... Fraser's work here is exciting, full of promise, intriguing images and sudden unexpected turns."

— Maureen Hynes, Poetry Spoken Here/
League of Canadian Poets

Fraser succeeds in drawing the reader in to her passionate telling, and leaves one with a powerful and authentic portrait of a family.

— Pagitica

Friendships, animosities, sexual encounters, and children are among the subjects explored in these graceful, finely tuned poems ... Fraser's poetry is full of startling metaphors ... She deploys these metaphors to crack open relationships of all kinds ...

— *Canadian Book Review Annual* 2001

RECYCLED
Paper made from
recycled material
FSC® C100212
FSC
www.fsc.org

Printed in June 2014
by Gauvin Press,
Gatineau, Québec